Tastes&Flavors
of MAUI

Tastes&Flavors
of MAUI

MUTUAL PUBLISHING

ISBN 1-56647-733-6
Library of Congress Catalog Card Number: 2005930352

Photograph on page 10, page 32, page 39, page 46, page 49, page 58, page 64, page
66 and page 70 cover and backcover by Ray Wong
All other photographs © Douglas Peebles

Design by Wanni

First Printing, October 2005
1 2 3 4 5 6 7 8 9

Mutual Publishing, LLC
1215 Center Street, Suite 210
Honolulu, Hawai'i 96816
Ph: 808-732-1709 / Fax: 808-734-4094
E-mail: mutual@mutualpublishing.com
www.mutualpublishing.com

Printed in Korea

Table of Contents

Entrées

Desserts

Beverages & Drinks

Glossary

Introduction

Maui No Ka ʻOi—"Maui is the best"—is a phrase coined by proud kamaʻāina who live on Maui, and surely all who experience this charming island would agree. It is a place that possesses everything one expects from a tropical island: unsurpassed beauty, extravagant resorts, miles of sunny beaches, towering mountain ranges, deep valleys and, last but not least, excellent restaurants renown for their fine dining and culinary offerings. The rise of culinary arts in Hawaiʻi began when a new generation of chefs emerged onto the local restaurant scene nearly a decade ago. Since then, dining in Hawaiʻi has never been quite the same. These progressive and experimental chefs fused traditional flavors to create contemporary ones; added a dose of fresh creativity to presentation; and took risks to make something new, something different. Most importantly, these chefs embraced the use of local fruits, produce, and seafood once not commonly used in Hawaiʻi's restaurants. The birth of Hawaiian Regional Cuisine had begun.

The influences of Hawaiian Regional Cuisine were far-reaching. What would have been considered "fine dining" in the past became more accessible to the local palate. Grabbing a "gourmet" plate lunch now meant Chinese five spice chicken with a side of macaroni salad or Waimānalo greens; enjoying pūpūs at pau hana meant having seared ʻahi with furikake with your martinis or Kona crab cakes with your beer.

Maui is certainly at the heart of Hawaiʻi's culinary renaissance. Since blending unique, local ingredients into a dish is a signature mark of Hawaiian Regional Cuisine, Maui—with its diverse agricultural industry—is certainly where some of the most creative cooking can take place. Fine Hawaiian coffees, sweet pineapples and the famous Kula onions among others, grace fields and fields of fertile Maui land. And the options keep expanding. Farmers recently started cultivating lavender on the upland slopes near Haleakalā and are now experimenting with olive trees (for olive oil), providing more unusual, local ingredients that add flair to cooking and feasting.

Tastes & Flavors of Maui is a slice of Maui's best. The collection of recipes in this little cookbook, while flavored with the gourmet touch, is still simple and fun to make. Whether you are cooking for one, or for friends and family, the dishes featured here will give all a taste of Maui.

TAPAS & APPETIZERS

Seared 'Ahi with Furikake

Serves 4 to 6 appetizer servings

1 pound 'ahi fillet, cut into 2 x 2-inch blocks
1/4 cup furikake for coating
2 to 3 teaspoons oil

Dipping Sauce
2 tablespoons soy sauce
Wasabi to taste

Coat 'ahi pieces with furikake. Sear 'ahi very quickly (5 to 8 seconds) on all sides in hot oil in nonstick skillet over medium-high heat, keeping the middle raw. Slice 'ahi sashimi style. Mix soy sauce and wasabi to desired taste and use as dipping sauce.

—Originally appeared in Hawai'i's Best Pūpū and Potluck

Crab Stuffed Shiitake Mushrooms with Dijon Dip

Serves 12 to 16

1 pound fresh shiitake mushrooms, cleaned and stems removed
3 tablespoons butter or margarine
1/4 cup chopped onion
1/4 cup chopped bell pepper
1/2 cup cooked crabmeat
1 cup bread crumbs
2 teaspoons chopped fresh or 1/2 teaspoon dried thyme leaves
1/4 teaspoon salt
1/4 teaspoon ground turmeric
1/4 teaspoon pepper

Finely chop mushroom stems to measure 1/3 cup. Heat 2 tablespoons butter in skillet over medium heat; cook mushroom stems, onion, and bell pepper in butter about 3 minutes, stirring occasionally; remove from heat. Stir in remaining ingredients. Cool.

Fill mushroom caps with crab mixture. Place mushrooms, filled sides up, on lightly sprayed baking pan. Bake in 350°F oven for 10 to12 minutes. Serve hot with Dijon Mustard Sauce.

Sweet Maui Onion Lomi Lomi Salmon

Serves 6 to 8

1/2 pound salted salmon
5 firm-ripe tomatoes, diced
10 green onion stalks, chopped
1 medium Maui onion*, chopped
Juice of 1 lemon
1 tablespoon chili pepper water, optional

Soak salmon for 2 hours in cold water. Remove any excess bones and skin, then cut into small cubes. Combine all ingredients and mix well. Chill and serve.

*Kula Maui onion preferred

Pipikaula
(Beef Jerky)

Makes about 3 pounds

4 pounds flank steak, cut into 2-inch wide strips

Marinade:
1 cup soy sauce
1/2 cup sake or dry sherry
2 teaspoons liquid smoke
3 tablespoons sugar
2 teaspoons salt
1/4 teaspoon black pepper
1 1/2-inch piece fresh ginger root, minced
2 cloves garlic, pressed
2 Hawaiian red peppers, seeded and minced

Combine all marinade ingredients in plastic bag; zip bag to close; shake to mix well. Marinate beef for 24 hours in refrigerator, turning several times. Drain meat and arrange on racks. Place on foil-lined shallow baking sheets. Oven dry meat at 200°F for 7 to 8 hours or until meat is the texture of "jerky." Meat may be stored for 5 days in the refrigerator or in the freezer for 6 to 8 months. Slice diagonally to serve hot or cold as pūpū or side dish.

—*Originally appeared in* Pūpū Party Planner

DRESSINGS & SAUCES

Papaya Seed Dressing

Makes 2 cups

1/4 cup crushed papaya seeds
2 tablespoons fresh rosemary or 2 teaspoons dried rosemary
1 tablespoon fresh tarragon or 1 teaspoon dried tarragon
1 clove garlic, minced
1 tablespoon lime zest, lemon zest or passion fruit pulp
1/3 cup red wine vinegar
2 cups salad oil, olive oil or macadamia nut oil

Place all ingredients, except the oil, into a large mixing bowl and stir to moisten. Using a wire whisk, slowly combine the oil with the dressing ingredients. Chill at least 1 hour before serving.

Dijon Mustard Dip

Makes 1 cup

1/2 cup sour cream
1/2 cup plain yogurt
1 tablespoon minced fresh parsley
3/4 teaspoon onion powder
1/2 teaspoon garlic salt
2 teaspoon Dijon mustard

Mix all ingredients together. Cover and refrigerate at least 1 hour before servings. May be served with meatballs, cocktail sausages, or crudités, if desired.

Maui Onion Salad Dressing

Makes 1 cup

1 clove garlic
1/2 Maui onion, sliced
1/2 cup canola oil
1 tablespoon Dijon mustard
2 teaspoons sugar
1/4 teaspoon rice vinegar
Salt and fresh ground pepper to taste

In food processor, mince garlic and Maui onion. Add remaining ingredients and blend thoroughly. Chill before serving.

—Originally appeared in Another Taste of Aloha

Teriyaki Sauce

Makes 3 cup

1-1/2 cups soy sauce
1/2 cup mirin or sake
1/2 cup water
Juice of 1 medium orange
1 cup brown sugar, packed
2 cloves garlic, crushed
2 teaspoons fresh ginger, minced

Combine all ingredients in a jar; cover and shake vigorously to combine. Keep in refrigerator if not using immediately. Use as a marinade or seasoning for Oriental dishes.

SOUPS &
SALADS

Moloka'i Sweet Potato Salad

Serves 6 to 10

4 medium Molokaʻi sweet potatoes
6 hard cooked eggs, chopped
1 stalk celery, chopped
1/2 Maui onion, chopped
1/4 cup sweet pickled relish
1 tablespoon parsley, chopped
1/2 cup mayonnaise
Salt and fresh ground pepper to taste

Garnish
Paprika
Parsley

Boil potatoes with skin in slightly salted water to cover until tender, not mushy. Cool, peel and cut into 1-inch cubes. Mix together eggs, celery, relish, and mayonnaise in a large bowl. Gently toss potatoes with egg mixture. Salt and pepper to taste. Chill 1 to 2 hours before serving. Garnish with paprika and parsley.

Mixed Hawaiian Fruit Salad

Serves 4

2 tablespoons honey
1/4 cup Cream Salad Dressing (see recipe below)
1/4 cup Hot Pepper Dressing (see recipe below)
1 cup crushed pineapple
1 cup sliced banana
1 cup diced papaya
1 cup melon pieces
Lettuce
Cayenne pepper or nutmeg to taste

Combine honey and dressings and let flavors infuse for about 1 hour in the refrigerator. Toss together fruit and arrange on lettuce and sprinkle with a little cayenne pepper or a little grated nutmeg. Serve with dressing.

Cream Salad Dressing
1/4 cup heavy whipping cream
1/8 teaspoon kosher salt
1 teaspoon granulated sugar
Pinch of black pepper
1 tablespoon white cider vinegar

Beat cream until it thickens. Stir in salt, sugar, and pepper and mix well. Slowly add and beat in the vinegar. Refrigerate.

Hot Pepper Dressing

2 tablespoons olive oil
2 tablespoons white cider vinegar
1/2 teaspoon salt
1/4 teaspoon cayenne pepper
1/8 teaspoon granulated sugar

Place ingredients in a small jar, cover tightly and chill thoroughly in the refrigerator. Shake vigorously for 1 to 2 minutes, just before serving.

—Originally appeared in Hawai'i's Favorite Pineapple Recipes

Maui Onion Soup

Serves 4 to 6

4 large Maui onions, sliced
4 cloves garlic, chopped
1/4 cup butter
1-1/2 quart beef stock or broth
2 ounces sherry wine
Salt and fresh ground pepper to taste
4–6 slices French bread
1/2 cup Swiss cheese, freshly grated
1/4 cup Parmesan cheese, freshly grated

Sauté Maui onions with butter in a medium stock pot. Stir occasionally over low heat until onions are dark brown. Add garlic and the beef stock or broth. Lower heat and simmer for 20 minutes. Salt and pepper to taste. Serve soup in individual bowls topped with a slice of French bread and Swiss cheese. Sprinkle top with Parmesan cheese. Place bowls on baking sheet and broil until cheese is golden brown. Remove from oven and serve immediately.

Portuguese Bean Soup

Serves 8 to 10

2 ham shanks
1 (12-ounce) package Portuguese sausage, cut into chunks
1 quart water
1 (8-ounce) can tomato sauce
1 large Maui onion, peeled and wedged
2 potatoes, peeled and cubed
1 carrot, peel and cubed
1-1/2 teaspoons salt
Dash of pepper
Dash of paprika, optional
2 (15-ounce) cans kidney beans.

Simmer ham shanks and sausage in water for 2 hours over medium heat. Add remaining ingredients; cook additional 20 to 30 minutes or until vegetables are tender. Serve hot with crackers or over steamed rice.

—*Originally appeared in* Maxi Meals for Mini Money

CHIPS 'N DIPS

Garlic Bread

Serves 6 to 8

6 cloves garlic, chopped
5 tablespoons butter, softened
2 tablespoons American parsley, finely chopped
1 loaf French bread, sliced
Parmesan cheese, freshly grated

Mix together chopped garlic, parsley and butter. Arrange
French bread on baking pan. Spread on the garlic mixture and
sprinkle with Parmesan cheese. Broil until golden brown.

Pineapple Confetti Salsa

Makes about 3 cups

2 cups diced fresh pineapple or canned pineapple chunks,
    well drained
1/4 cup red onion, diced
1/4 cup yellow bell pepper, diced
1/4 cup green bell pepper, diced
2 tablespoons raisins, chopped
1 teaspoon garlic, minced
1 jalapeño pepper, seeded and minced
1/2 teaspoon ground coriander
1/4 teaspoon ground cumin
1/8 teaspoon kosher salt

Garnish
2 Roma tomatoes, seeded and diced

In a medium bowl, fold together pineapple, onion, bell peppers, raisins, and garlic; set aside. In a cup, combine jalapeño, coriander, cumin, and salt; mix well and sprinkle over pineapple mixture. Toss until spices are evenly distributed. Cover and refrigerate overnight. Garnish with diced tomatoes.

—Originally appeared in Hawai'i's Favorite Pineapple Recipes

Taro and Sweet Potato Chips

Taro Root, cleaned and peeled
Sweet Potato, cleaned and peeled
Canola or vegetable oil for deep-frying

Slice taro root and sweet potato thinly with slicer. Dry well
and fry in oil heated to 350-375°F until golden brown. Drain
on absorbent paper and salt before serving. Chips may be
frozen or stored in airtight containers.

Pickled Maui Onions

Makes about 1 gallon

1 quart red wine or white vinegar
1 quart water
1/3 cup Hawaiian rock salt
1/2 cup sugar
4 pounds Maui onions, quartered
2 to 3 large carrots, sliced
1 large green pepper, sliced

Combine vinegar, water, salt, and sugar in a saucepan and bring it to a boil. Place onions, carrots, and green pepper in a gallon jar; pour vinegar mixture over; let cool. Cover and refrigerate for 2 to 3 weeks before serving.

Maui Onion Dip

Serves 4 to 6

1 small Maui onion, finely chopped
16 ounces sour cream
1/2 cup mayonnaise
4 teaspoons chives, chopped
1/4 teaspoon garlic powder
Salt and fresh ground white pepper to taste

Combine all ingredients in a mixing bowl; mix well. Chill before serving.

Creamy Crab Dip

Serves 4 to 6

8 ounces cream cheese
1 teaspoon milk
2 teaspoons Worcestershire sauce
1/2 pound imitation crab, shredded
2 teaspoons green onions, chopped
1/4 cup Parmesan cheese, grated
Salt and fresh ground pepper to taste

Mix together cream cheese, milk, and Worcestershire sauce; stir in the crab meat and green onions. Salt and pepper to taste. Place dip in heat-resistant dish. Bake in 350 °F for 10 minutes. Sprinkle Parmesan cheese on top. Serve with broccoli, celery, carrot sticks, or Maui Potato Chips.

ENTRÉES

Kālua Turkey

Serves 10 to 12

18- to 20-pound turkey
2 handfuls Hawaiian salt
1/2 bottle liquid smoke
2 to 3 tī leaves, washed and ribs removed
Heavy-duty aluminum foil

Remove neck, giblets and heart from turkey cavity. Wash turkey well with cold water; drain and pat dry. Line roasting pan with aluminum foil. Place turkey on foil; rub inside cavity and outside well with Hawaiian salt. Pour liquid smoke inside and outside of turkey. Cover with tī leaves then with aluminum foil, sealing all edges securely around pan. Bake 350°F for 2 hours. Lower oven temperature to 225 °F and bake an additional 5 hours; let rest 30 minutes before shredding turkey meat from the bones. Add more Hawaiian salt or sea salt and liquid smoke to pan juices if needed. Place shredded turkey in another pan and pour juices over turkey and enjoy.

Cold Ginger Chicken

Serves 2 to 4

4 skinless chicken breasts
1 (14-1/2 ounce) can chicken broth
Ginger Sauce (see recipe below)

In medium saucepan, bring chicken broth to a boil. Add chicken and bring to a boil; reduce heat and simmer for 6 to 8 minutes. Remove chicken and refrigerate to chill. Cut chicken into desired pieces and arrange on platter. Top with cold Ginger Sauce.

Ginger Sauce
1/4 cup canola oil
1/4 cup fresh ginger, finely chopped
2 tablespoons cilantro, chopped
2 tablespoons green onions, finely chopped
1 teaspoon soy sauce
Salt to taste

Heat canola oil to smoking point; add grated ginger (be careful of splattering). Let cool and add remaining ingredients. Season with salt to taste.

Homestyle Chicken

Serves 16

5 pounds chicken pieces
1/3 cup ketchup
1/3 cup soy sauce
1/2 cup brown sugar
3 tablespoons sherry
1 piece ginger root, crushed
1 clove garlic, crushed

Arrange chicken, skin side up, on rack of broiler pan. Broil 6 to 8 inches from unit heating for 10 minutes on each side. Combine remaining ingredients; baste chicken and continue broiling for 10 more minutes on each side, basting frequently with sauce.

Curried Mahimahi

Serves 4

1 pound mahimahi fillet (ono or snapper may be substituted)
1 egg, beaten
1 cup bread or cornflakes crumbs
Canola or vegetable oil for frying

Marinade
1 tablespoon sugar
1 teaspoon salt
1 tablespoon mirin or dry sherry
2 teaspoons curry powder
2 tablespoons cornstarch
1 tablespoon soy sauce

Slice fish fillet into serving pieces. Combine all Marinade
ingredients; mix to blend well; marinate fish 30 minutes or
longer. Dip fillets in egg then dredge in bread crumbs. Pan-fry
in hot oil for 1 to 2 minutes on each side or until golden
brown. Drain on absorbent paper and serve immediately with
hot steamed rice.

Mochiko Chicken with Garlic Dipping Sauce

Serves 6 to 8

4 pounds chicken thighs or wings

Marinade
2 tablespoons flour
1/4 cup cornstarch
1/4 cup mochiko
1/4 cup sugar
1-1/2 teaspoons salt
1/3 cup soy sauce
1 teaspoon oyster sauce
2 eggs, beaten
2 tablespoons green onions, finely chopped
1 tablespoon toasted sesame seeds

Mix all marinade ingredients together. Add chicken and marinate for 2 hours. Pan-fry in hot oil until brown and done.

Garlic Dipping Sauce
1/2 cup soy sauce
1/4 cup rice vinegar
1/4 cup sugar
2 tablespoons garlic, pressed
1 tablespoon fresh ginger, grated
1 teaspoon chili sauce
1 teaspoon sesame oil

Garnish
3 green onion stalks, sliced

Mix together all ingredients. Serve with hot chicken by dipping or sprinkling.

—Originally appeared in Favorite Island Cookery Book 1

Spicy Sweet and Sour Shrimp

Serves 4 to 6

1 pound fresh or frozen shrimp, peeled and deveined
1 cup teriyaki sauce
1/3 cup pineapple juice
1 tablespoon rice vinegar
1/4 teaspoon hot sauce
1/4 teaspoon cornstarch
2 teaspoons canola oil
1 teaspoon fresh ginger, peeled and minced
1 cup fresh pineapple chunks
2 tablespoons green onions, minced
2 cups long beans or fresh young green beans,
    cut into 1-1/2-inch lengths

Garnish
Toasted sesame seeds

Whisk together teriyaki sauce, pineapple juice, vinegar and hot sauce; blend in cornstarch and set aside. In a saucepan, heat oil and sauté ginger. Add pineapple chunks and green onions; cook until pineapple begins to brown, stirring occasionally. Add teriyaki-pineapple mixture and beans. Simmer for about 5 minutes over medium heat. In a separate heavy skillet or wok, sauté shrimp in hot oil until they turn pink. Add to sauce and remove from heat. Serve over a bed of steamed rice and garnish with toasted sesame seeds.

—*Originally appeared in* Hawai'i's Favorite Pineapple Recipes

Traditional Soy Sauce Chicken

Serves 6 to 8

12 chicken thighs, skinless
2 cups soy sauce
2 cups water
2 cloves garlic, smashed
1 cup brown sugar, packed
1 teaspoon fresh ginger, grated

Heat soy sauce, ginger, water and sugar in a large pot until sugar dissolves. Add chicken, and bring to a boil; reduce heat and simmer for 30 to 45 minutes or until tender. Serve with steamed rice.

DESSERTS

Traditional Haupia

Makes about 32 (2 x 2-inch) pieces

4 cups coconut milk
1 cup water
1 cup cornstarch
1 cup sugar

In a large saucepan combine all ingredients; stir until cornstarch dissolves. Cook over medium heat, stirring constantly, until mixture comes to a boil. Reduce heat and cook until mixture thickens. Pour into two 8-inch square pans and chill until firm. Cut into desired pieces to serve.

Kula Raspberry Cream Cheese Pie

Serves 6 to 8

1 (8-inch) graham cracker crust
1 (8-ounce) package cream cheese, softened
1 (14-ounce) can sweetened condensed milk
1/3 cup lemon juice from concentrate
1 teaspoon almond extract
1 pint basket raspberries, washed and picked over

Glaze
1/4 cup red currant jelly, melted

In a large bowl, whisk together softened cream cheese and sweetened condensed milk. Once blended, stir in lemon juice and almond extract. Pour into graham cracker crust and chill overnight or until set, about 4 hours.

Just before serving arrange raspberries over top of pie; brush with red currant glaze.

Coconut Pound Cake

Serves 10 to 12

1 cup butter, softened
1/2 cup vegetable shortening
3 cups sugar
1/4 teaspoon salt
6 eggs
1 teaspoon lemon juice
1 teaspoon vanilla
1 teaspoon almond flavoring
1 teaspoon coconut flavoring
3 cups all-purpose flour, sifted
1 cup milk
1 (3-1/2-ounce) can flaked coconut

Preheat oven to 325 °F. Cream butter, sugar, and shortening until light and fluffy. Add eggs, one at a time, beating well after each addition. Add flavorings, flour, and milk, alternating flour and milk, about one-third at a time. Fold in coconut. Pour batter into a greased tube pan. Bake at 350°F for about 1-1/2 hours. This cake keeps well in the refrigerator. It also freezes well.

Maui An Mochi

Serves 18

2-1/2 cups mochiko flour
1-1/4 cups brown sugar
1 teaspoon baking powder
1 (12-ounce) can coconut milk
2 cups water
3/4 cup koshian

Mix all ingredients until smooth and well blended. Pour into large, greased microwave tube pan. Microwave medium high for 15 minutes. Cool.

Maui Yaki Manju

Makes about 18 to 24

2-1/2 cups all-purpose flour
3 tablespoons sugar
1/2 teaspoons salt
1 cup salad oil
6 tablespoons ice-cold water
1 cup tsubushi an

Mix together dry ingredients. Add oil and water; mix well.
From about 1 generous tablespoon dough and form into ball;
flatten and place 1 teaspoon "an" in center; pinch edges of
dough together to seal. Place on lightly sprayed cookie sheet,
seam side down. Bake at 400°F 35 to 40 minutes or until
golden brown.

—*Originally appeared in* Cook Japanese

Orange Pound Cake

Serves 10 to 12

1 cup butter or margarine
2 cups sugar
5 eggs
3 cups all-purpose flour, sifted
3 teaspoons baking powder
1/4 teaspoon salt
3/4 cup fresh orange juice*
Zest of one orange, grated

Glaze
1/4 cup butter or margarine
1/3 cup bourbon
2/3 cup sugar

Combine ingredients for glaze in a saucepan and heat until the sugar is dissolved. DO NOT LET BOIL. Set aside until cake is baked.

Cream margarine and sugar until light and fluffy. Beat in eggs one at a time, beating well after each addition. Sift dry ingredients together and add to batter alternately with orange juice, ending with orange juice. Add orange zest. Pour into a greased and floured tube pan. Bake at 350°F for 1 hour. Prick the top of the cake with a fork then pour glaze evenly over the cake. Leave in the pan until thoroughly cooled. This cake can be made ahead of time and frozen, or kept in the refrigerator until ready to serve.

*Cannot substitute with frozen orange juice.

—Originally appeared in Maui Cooks

Maui Pineapple Upside-down Cake

Serves 8 to 10

3/4 cup brown sugar, packed
1/2 cup butter, divided
1/2 to 1 fresh pineapple*
1 cup granulated sugar
1 egg, beaten
1-1/2 cups cake flour or 1-1/4 cups all-purpose flour
2 teaspoons baking powder
1/8 teaspoon salt
3/4 cup pineapple juice

In a small bowl, beat together brown sugar and 2 tablespoons butter until mixture is well blended and creamy.

Spray a 9-inch cake pan with vegetable spray and press the sugar mixture against the sides and bottom of the cake pan. Cover bottom of pan with pineapple rings or pieces and press into the sugar mixture, making sure that the pineapple pieces cover the entire bottom of the pan.

Combine the remaining butter and granulated sugar and beat until light and fluffy; add egg and blend well. In a medium bowl, sift together the cake flour, baking powder, and salt. Fold into mixture. Add pineapple juice until mixture is well blended.

Pour batter into the fruit-lined cake pan. Bake at 350°F for about 40 to 45 minutes or until done. Let rest 15 minutes then turn cake out onto serving platter. Serve warm.

*Substitution: 1 can of sliced pineapple.

—Originally appeared in Hawai'i's Favorite Pineapple Recipes

Crispy Mango Cobbler

Serves 8 to 10

5 large mangoes*, cut into bite-size pieces
2 tablespoons lemon juice
2 tablespoons brown or raw sugar
2 tablespoons butter
2 tablespoons flour

Topping
1 block butter, slightly softened
1 cup flour
1 cup brown or raw sugar
1/2 cup macadamia nuts**, chopped

Mix first five ingredients and toss together; transfer into a casserole dish.

To prepare topping, cut the flour into the butter until "mealy" in texture; add the remaining ingredients. If topping is too soft, place in refrigerator 15 to 20 minutes to harden then crumble with hands over the mangoes. Bake in 400 °F oven until brown and bubbling, about 25 to 30 minutes.

Notes: May need to place another pan underneath to catch the overflow.

*Fruit substitutions: peaches, apples, papaya
**Nut substitutions: pecans, almonds

BEVERAGES & DRINKS

Orange-Mango Shake

Serves 2

1 medium-size ripe mango*, peeled, seeded and chopped
1 cup orange juice
1/2 teaspoon vanilla extract
1 cup vanilla ice cream, softened
1 cup ice cubes

Combine all ingredients in a blender and blend until smooth.

*Substitutions:
1 cup fresh strawberries for mango
Pineapple juice for orange juice
Pineapple sherbet for ice cream

Banana Smoothie

Serves 2 to 3

Ice cold water
4 frozen bananas*, peeled and sliced
1 tablespoon maple syrup
1 teaspoon vanilla

In a blender, start with one cup of ice cold water. Add the remaining ingredients and blend. If too thick, add more water. Sweeten to taste.

*Substitutions:
Strawberries, carob or carob-mint for bananas

Tropical Iced Tea

Serves 6 to 8

1/2 gallon water
12 black tea bags
3 sprigs fresh mint
2 cups sugar
12 ounces pineapple juice
6 ounces lemon juice

Garnishes
Pineapple spears
Fresh mint sprigs

In a large pot, bring water to a boil. Steep the tea bags and fresh mint in the hot water. Remove the mint after 3 minutes but continue to steep the tea until it is very dark. Remove tea bags. Add sugar and juices while tea is still warm. Stir to dissolve sugar. Pour into a gallon container and add water to fill. Refrigerate. Serve with ice and garnishes.

Haleakalā Sunrise

Serves 1

2 ounces light rum
2 ounces pineapple juice, unsweetened
2 ounces orange juice
2 ounces guava juice
3/4 ounce grenadine syrup
Ice cubes

Combine rum, fruit juices, and ice cubes. Stir. Fill large glass with ice. Strain rum mixture into glass. Pour in grenadine slowly. Allow to settle. Just before serving, stir slightly. The effect will be that of a sunrise at the Haleakala Crater on Maui.

—*Originally appeared in* Cooking with Aloha

Li Hing Pineapple Margarita

Serves 1

1 lime wedge for coating rim of glass
Kosher salt and Li Hing powder for coating rim of glass
1-1/4 ounces tequila
2 ounces Sweet & Sour Margarita Mix (see recipe below)
1/8 cup crushed pineapple
1/2 ounce Simple Syrup (see recipe below)
1/2 teaspoon Li Hing powder
5 ice cubes

Rub the rim of a margarita glass with a lime wedge and dip the rim in kosher salt and Li Hing powder to lightly coat. Chill the glass. In a blender, blend remaining ingredients, including ice cubes, for 30 seconds. Pour slurry into a chilled glass and serve.

Simple Syrup
2 cups granulated sugar
5 cups water

In a large saucepan, combine water and sugar and stir over medium heat until sugar dissolves. Bring to a simmer and then cool.

Sweet & Sour Mix
1/4 cup fresh lemon juice
1/4 cup granulated sugar

In a small saucepan, combine lemon juice and sugar and stir over medium heat until sugar dissolves. Remove from heat and cool.

—Originally appeared in Hawai'i's Favorite Pineapple Recipes

The Original Mai Tai

Serves 1

1-1/2 ounces Myers's Plantation rum*
1 ounce Cuban rum
3/4 ounce fresh lime juice
1/4 ounce Falernum
1/2 ounce Cointreau
2 dashes Angostura bitters
1 dash Pernod
Shell of squeezed lime
1 cup of cracked ice (size of a dime)

Pour all ingredients into a mixer and shake for 1 minute on medium speed. Serve in a double old-fashioned glass. Garnish with four sprigs of mint. Add a spear of pineapple. Sip slowly through mint sprigs until desired effect results.

*Recommended rum substitutions:
1-1/2 ounces Appleton Estate
1 ounce British Navy-style rum such as Pusser's or Lamb's

Glossary

A

'Ahi:
Hawaiian name for yellowfin or bigeye tuna. Also called shibi in Japanese. When the term 'ahi is used, it is assumed that fresh tuna, rather than canned, is meant.

C

Coconut milk:
The liquid extracted by squeezing the grated meat of a coconut; most often found in canned and frozen forms.

F

Furikake:
A condiment for rice made with shredded and seasoned dried seaweed and fish flakes.

H

Haupia:
Hawaiian name given to coconut pudding, but now often used for many coconut-flavored desserts.

Hawaiian salt:
White coarse sea salt.

K

Kālua:
Usually refers to a whole pig cooked in an imu, or underground oven. Substitution: turkey.

L

Lomi lomi salmon:
A fresh-tasting Hawaiian salad of salt-cured salmon, onion, and tomato.

M

Macadamia nuts:
Rich, slightly sweet nuts that are a major crop in Hawai'i; often called "Mac Nuts."

Mahimahi:
Dolphinfish with firm, pink flesh.

Mango:
A sweet, flavorful, and aromatic fruit when ripe. Varieties range from greenish-yellow to red in color when ripe with yellow to bright orange flesh. They range 1/4 to 2 pounds and may be smooth or fibrous in texture. Hayden mangoes have a slightly fibrous pulp.

Manju:
    A baked or steamed sweet bean filled bun.

Maui onion:
    Large white onion noted for its sweet flavor, usually grown in Kula, the upcountry region of Maui. Substitute with other sweet onions, such as Vidalia or Texas.

Mirin:
    Sweet Japanese rice wine.

Mochiko flour:
    Japanese glutinous rice flour used in making pastries and some sauces.

Moloka'i sweet potato:
    Grown in small quantities on the island of Moloka'i. Substitute any sweet potatoes.

O

Ono:
    Mackerel with white, firm flesh. Also known as waihoo.

Oyster sauce:
    A concentrated dark-brown sauce made from oysters, salt and soy sauce. Used in many Asian dishes to impart a full, rich flavor.

P

Papaya:
    The most common papaya used in Hawai'i is the solo papaya, a tropical fruit with a yellow flesh, black seeds and a perfumey scent. Other types are larger, and may have pink flesh; all are suitable for island recipes.

Passion fruit:
    A common variety of this fruit in Hawai'i has a yellow, shiny outer shell filled inside with seeds surrounded with a juicy pulp. This juice is tangy and unique in flavor. It is also known as liliko'i.

Pineapple:
    Fresh pineapples are covered with a prickly, brown skin, and topped with sharp, pointed leaves. To select a fresh ripe pineapple, give the tiny center leaves at the top a light tug. The leaves will easily pluck out of a ripe pineapple. Fresh pineapple contains an enzyme which will break down protein; rinse well and add as close to serving time as possible when using in dishes containing gelatin.

R

Rice vinegar:
    A type of vinegar made from rice wine; generally clear with a pale straw color. Generally, rice vinegar is mellow and lower in acid than other vinegars.

S

Sake:
Japanese rice wine.

Sesame oil:
Oil pressed from the sesame seed is available in two forms. Pressing the raw seed produces an oil, which is light in color and flavor and can be used for a wide variety of purposes. When the oil is pressed from toasted sesame seeds, it is dark in color with a much stronger flavor. It is this darker version that is to be used in the recipes of this book.

Sesame seeds:
The edible seeds of a plant of the Pedaliaceae family that have a distinctive nutty flavor. They come in black or white varieties, and are known as benne seeds and goma.

Shoyu:
Japanese terminology for soy sauce.

T

Tapas:
A cultural term for appetizers, or pūpū, popularly consumed in bars and restaurants in Spain, and usually enjoyed with sherry or other types of cocktails. Tapas range from simple to elaborate, such as olives and cubes of cheese to cold omelets and spicy snails; can be served as an entire meal also.

Teriyaki Sauce:
Japanese sauce or marinade with soy sauce, sugar and fresh ginger.

Ti leaves:
The leaves of the ti plant. Used to steam and bake fish and vegetables. Often called "Hawaiian aluminum foil." Substitute banana leaves, grape leaves or even corn husks. Available at wholesale florist shops.

Tsubushi an:
Coarsely mashed sweetened red azuki bean paste

W

Wasabi:
Also called Japanese horseradish; comes in both powder and paste forms. It is pale green in color, and produces a sharp, tingling sensation in the nose and palate.